Air Fryer Recipe Book

Recipes for Smart People

By

Caroline Taylor

Table of content

Ahi Tuna with Peppers and Tartare Sauce

(Ready in about 15 minutes | Servings 2)

Per serving:

485 Calories; 24.3g Fat; 7.7g Carbs; 56.3g Protein; 3g Sugars

Ingredients

2 ahi tuna steaks

2 Spanish peppers, quartered 1 teaspoon olive oil

1/2 teaspoon garlic powder

Salt and freshly ground black pepper, to taste Tartare sauce:

4 tablespoons mayonnaise 2 tablespoons sour cream

1 tablespoon baby capers, drained

1 tablespoon gherkins, drained and chopped 2 tablespoons white onion, minced

Directions

Pat the ahi tuna dry using kitchen towels.

Toss the ahi tuna and Spanish peppers with olive oil, garlic powder, salt and black pepper.

Cook the ahi tuna and peppers in the preheated Air Fryer at 400 degrees F for 10 minutes, flipping them halfway through the cooking time.

Meanwhile, whisk all the sauce Ingredients until well combined. Plate the ahi tuna steaks and arrange Spanish peppers around them. Serve with tartare sauce on the side and enjoy!

Anchovy and Cheese Wontons

(Ready in about 15 minutes | Servings 2)

Per serving:

473 Calories; 25.1g Fat; 19.4g Carbs; 41g Protein; 4.9g Sugars

Ingredients

1/2 pound anchovies

1/2 cup cheddar cheese, grated 1 cup fresh spinach

2 tablespoons scallions, minced 1 teaspoon garlic, minced

1 tablespoon Shoyu sauce

Himalayan salt and ground black pepper, to taste 1/2 pound wonton wrappers

1 teaspoon sesame oil

Directions

Mash the anchovies and mix with the cheese, spinach, scallions, garlic and Shoyu sauce; season with salt and black pepper and mix to combine well.

Fill your wontons with 1 tablespoon of the filling mixture and fold into triangle shape; brush the side with a bit of oil and water to seal the edges.

Cook in your Air Fryer at 390 degrees F for 10 minutes, flipping the wontons for even cooking. Enjoy!

Asian-Style Beef Dumplings

(Ready in about 25 minutes | Servings 5)

Per serving:

353 Calories; 16.7g Fat; 29.5g Carbs; 23.1g Protein; 3.4g Sugars

Ingredients

1/2 pound ground chuck

1/2 pound beef sausage, chopped 1 cup Chinese cabbage, shredded 1 bell pepper, chopped

1 onion, chopped

2 garlic cloves, minced

1 medium-sized egg, beaten

Sea salt and ground black pepper, to taste 20 wonton wrappers

2 tablespoons soy sauce 2 teaspoons sesame oil

2 teaspoons sesame seeds, lightly toasted

2 tablespoons seasoned rice vinegar 1/2 teaspoon chili sauce

Directions

To make the filling, thoroughly combine the ground chuck, sausage, cabbage, bell pepper, onion, garlic, egg, salt, and black pepper.

Place the wrappers on a clean and dry surface. Now, divide the filling among the wrappers.

Then, fold each dumpling in half and pinch to seal.

Transfer the dumplings to the lightly greased cooking basket. Bake at 390 degrees F for 15 minutes, turning over halfway through.

In the meantime, mix the soy sauce, sesame oil, sesame seeds, rice vinegar, and chili sauce. Serve the beef dumplings with the sauce on the side. Enjoy!

Beef Nuggets with Cheesy Mushrooms

(Ready in about 25 minutes | Servings 4)

Per serving:

355 Calories; 15.7g Fat; 13.6g Carbs; 39.8g Protein; 3.4g Sugars

Ingredients

2 eggs, beaten

4 tablespoons yogurt

1 cup tortilla chips, crushed

1 teaspoon dry mesquite flavored seasoning mix Coarse salt and ground black pepper, to taste 1/2 teaspoon onion powder

1 pound cube steak, cut into bite-size pieces 1 pound button mushrooms

1 cup Swiss cheese, shredded

Directions

In a shallow bowl, beat the eggs and yogurt. In a resealable bag, mix the tortilla chips, mesquite seasoning, salt, pepper, and onion powder.

Dip the steak pieces in the egg mixture; then, place in the bag, and shake to coat on all sides.

Cook at 400 degrees F for 14 minutes, flipping halfway through the cooking time.

Add the mushrooms to the lightly greased cooking basket. Top with shredded Swiss cheese.

Bake in the preheated Air Fryer at 400 degrees F for 5 minutes. Serve with the beef nuggets. Bon appétit!

Beef Schnitzel with Buttermilk Spaetzle

(Ready in about 20 minutes | Servings 2)

Per serving:

522 Calories; 20.7g Fat; 17.1g Carbs; 62.2g Protein; 1.8g Sugars

Ingredients

1 egg, beaten

1/2 teaspoon ground black pepper 1 teaspoon paprika

1/2 teaspoon coarse sea salt 1 tablespoon ghee, melted

1/2 cup tortilla chips, crushed

2 thin-cut minute steaks Buttermilk Spaetzle:

2 eggs

1/2 cup buttermilk

1/2 cup all-purpose flour 1/2 teaspoon salt

Directions

Start by preheating your Air Fryer to 360 degrees F.

In a shallow bowl, whisk the egg with black pepper, paprika, and salt.

Thoroughly combine the ghee with the crushed tortilla chips and coarse sea salt in another shallow bowl.

Using a meat mallet, pound the schnitzel to 1/4-inch thick.

Dip the schnitzel into the egg mixture; then, roll the schnitzel over the crumb mixture until coated on all sides.

Cook for 13 minutes in the preheated Air Fryer.

To make the spaetzle, whisk the eggs, buttermilk, flour, and salt in a bowl. Bring a large saucepan of salted water to a boil.

Push the spaetzle mixture through the holes of a potato ricer into the boiling water; slice them off using a table knife. Work in batches.

When the spaetzle float, take them out with a slotted spoon. Repeat with the rest of the spaetzle mixture.

Serve with warm schnitzel. Enjoy!

Beef Sausage Goulash

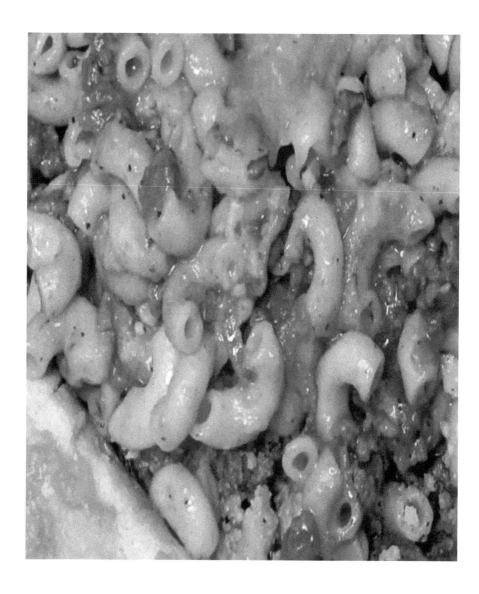

(Ready in about 40 minutes | Servings 2)

Per serving:

565 Calories; 47.1g Fat; 14.3g Carbs; 20.6g Protein; 5.2g Sugars

Ingredients

1 tablespoon lard, melted 1 shallot, chopped

1 bell pepper, chopped

2 red chilies, finely chopped 1 teaspoon ginger-garlic paste Sea salt, to taste

1/4 teaspoon ground black pepper

4 beef good quality sausages, thinly sliced 2 teaspoons smoked paprika

1 cup beef bone broth 1/2 cup tomato puree

2 handfuls spring greens, shredded

Directions

Melt the lard in a Dutch oven over medium-high flame; sauté the shallots and peppers about 4 minutes or until fragrant.

Add the ginger-garlic paste and cook an additional minute. Season with salt and black pepper and transfer to a lightly greased baking pan.

Then, brown the sausages, stirring occasionally, working in batches. Add to the baking pan.

Add the smoked paprika, broth, and tomato puree. Lower the pan onto the Air Fryer basket. Bake at 325 degrees F for 30 minutes.

Stir in the spring greens and cook for 5 minutes more or until they wilt. Serve over the hot rice if desired. Bon appétit!

Classic Calamari with Mediterranean Sauce

(Ready in about 10 minutes | Servings 2)

Per serving:

529 Calories; 24.3g Fat; 41g Carbs; 33.2g Protein; 3.2g Sugars

23

Ingredients

1/2 pound calamari tubes cut into rings, cleaned Sea salt and ground black pepper, to season

1/2 cup almond flour

1/2 cup all-purpose flour

4 tablespoons parmesan cheese, grated 1/2 cup ale beer

1/4 teaspoon cayenne pepper 1/2 cup breadcrumbs

1/4 cup mayonnaise

1/4 cup Greek-style yogurt 1 clove garlic, minced

1 tablespoon fresh lemon juice

1 teaspoon fresh parsley, chopped 1 teaspoon fresh dill, chopped

Directions

Sprinkle the calamari with salt and black pepper.

Mix the flour, cheese and beer in a bowl until well combined. In another bowl, mix cayenne pepper and breadcrumbs

Dip the calamari pieces in the flour mixture, then roll them onto the breadcrumb mixture, pressing to coat on all sides; transfer them to a lightly oiled cooking basket.

Cook at 400 degrees F for 4 minutes, shaking the basket halfway through the cooking time.

Meanwhile, mix the remaining Ingredients until everything is well incorporated. Serve warm calamari with the sauce for dipping. Enjoy!

Classic Crab Cakes

(Ready in about 15 minutes | Servings 3)

Per serving:

180 Calories; 4.4g Fat; 10.5g Carbs; 24.4g Protein; 3g Sugars

Ingredients

1 egg, beaten

2 tablespoons milk

2 crustless bread slices 1 pound lump crabmeat

2 tablespoons scallions, chopped 1 garlic clove, minced

1 teaspoon deli mustard

1 teaspoon Sriracha sauce

Sea salt and ground black pepper, to taste 4 lemon wedges, for serving

Directions

Whisk the egg and milk until pale and frothy; add in the bread and let it soak for a few minutes.

Stir in the other Ingredients, except for the lemon wedges; shape the mixture into 4 equal patties. Place your patties in the Air Fryer cooking basket. Spritz your patties with a nonstick cooking spray.

Cook the crab cakes at 400 degrees F for 5 minutes. Turn them over and cook on the other side for 5 minutes.

Serve warm, garnished with lemon wedges. Bon appétit!

Classic Fish Tacos

(Ready in about 15 minutes | Servings 3)

Per serving:

266 Calories; 10.8g Fat; 17.3g Carbs; 25.7g Protein; 2.6g Sugars

Ingredients

1 pound codfish

1 tablespoon olive oil

1 teaspoon Cajun spice mix Salt and red pepper, to taste 3 corn tortillas

1/2 avocado, pitted and diced 1 cup purple cabbage

1 jalapeño, minced

Directions

Pat the codfish dry with paper towels; toss the codfish with olive oil, Cajun spice mix, salt and black pepper.

Cook your codfish at 400 degrees F for 5 to 6 minutes. Then, turn the fish over and cook on the other side for 6 minutes until they are opaque.

Let the fish rest for 5 minutes before flaking with a fork.

Assemble the tacos: place the flaked fish over warmed tortillas; top with avocado, purple cabbage and minced jalapeño. Enjoy!

Classic Old Bay Fish with Cherry Tomatoes

(Ready in about 15 minutes | Servings 3)

Per serving:

291 Calories; 13.5g Fat; 10.4g Carbs; 31.9g Protein; 6.8g Sugars

Ingredients

1 pound swordfish steak 1/2 cup cornflakes, crushed

1 teaspoon Old Bay seasoning

Salt and black pepper, to season 2 teaspoon olive oil

1 pound cherry tomatoes

Directions

Toss the swordfish steak with cornflakes, Old Bay seasoning, salt, black pepper and 1 teaspoon of olive oil.

Cook the swordfish steak in your Air Fryer at 400 degrees F for 6 minutes.

Now, turn the fish over, top with tomatoes and drizzle with the remaining teaspoon of olive oil. Continue to cook for 4 minutes.

Serve with lemon slices if desired. Bon appétit!

Classic Pancetta-Wrapped Scallops

(Ready in about 10 minutes | Servings 3)

Per serving:

403 Calories; 24.5g Fat; 5.1g Carbs; 40.1g Protein; 3.1g Sugars

Ingredients

1 pound sea scallops

1 tablespoon deli mustard 2 tablespoons soy sauce

1/4 teaspoon shallot powder 1/4 teaspoon garlic powder 1/2 teaspoon dried dill

Sea salt and ground black pepper, to taste 4 ounces pancetta slices

Directions

Pat dry the sea scallops and transfer them to a mixing bowl. Toss the sea scallops with the deli mustard, soy sauce, shallot powder, garlic powder, dill, salt and black pepper.

Wrap a slice of bacon around each scallop and transfer them to the Air Fryer cooking basket.

Cook in your Air Fryer at 400 degrees F for 4 minutes; turn them over and cook an additional 3 minutes.

Serve with hot sauce for dipping if desired. Bon appétit!

Colorful Salmon and Fennel Salad

(Ready in about 20 minutes | Servings 3)

Per serving:

306 Calories; 16.3g Fat; 5.6g Carbs; 32.2g Protein; 3g Sugars

Ingredients

1 pound salmon

1 fennel, quartered 1 teaspoon olive oil

Sea salt and ground black pepper, to taste 1/2 teaspoon paprika

1 tablespoon balsamic vinegar

1 tablespoon lime juice

1 tablespoon extra-virgin olive oil 1 tomato, sliced

1 cucumber, sliced

1 tablespoon sesame seeds, lightly toasted

Directions

Toss the salmon and fennel with 1 teaspoon of olive oil, salt, black pepper and paprika.

Cook in the preheated Air Fryer at 380 degrees F for 12 minutes; shaking the basket once or twice.

Cut the salmon into bite-sized strips and transfer them to a nice salad bowl.

Add in the fennel, balsamic vinegar, lime juice, 1 tablespoon of extra-virgin olive oil, tomato and cucumber.

Toss to combine well and serve garnished with lightly toasted sesame seeds. Enjoy!

Dijon Catfish with Eggplant Sauce

(Ready in about 30 minutes | Servings 3)

Per serving:

336 Calories; 16.9g Fat; 18.6g Carbs; 28.2g Protein; 12.1g Sugars

Ingredients

1 pound catfish fillets

Sea salt and ground black pepper, to taste 1/4 cup Dijon mustard

1 tablespoon honey

1 tablespoon white vinegar

1 pound eggplant, 1 ½-inch cubes 2 tablespoons olive oil

1 tablespoon tahini

1/2 teaspoon garlic, minced

1 tablespoon parsley, chopped

Directions

Pat the catfish dry with paper towels and generously season with salt and black pepper.

In a small mixing bowl, thoroughly combine Dijon mustard, honey and vinegar.

Cook the fish in your Air Fryer at 400 degrees F for 5 minutes. Turn the fish over and brush with the Dijon mixture; continue to cook for a further 5 minutes.

Then, set your Air Fryer to 400 degrees F. Add the eggplant chunks to the cooking basket and cook for 15 minutes, shaking the basket occasionally to ensure even cooking.

Transfer the cooked eggplant to a bowl of your food processor; stir in the remaining Ingredients and blitz until everything is well blended and smooth.

Serve the warm catfish with the eggplant sauce on the side. Bon appétit!

Easiest Lobster Tails Ever

(Ready in about 10 minutes | Servings 2)

Per serving:

147 Calories; 3.5g Fat; 2.5g Carbs; 25.5g Protein; 1.1g Sugars

Ingredients

2 (6-ounce) lobster tails

1 teaspoon fresh cilantro, minced 1/2 teaspoon dried rosemary

1/2 teaspoon garlic, pressed 1 teaspoon deli mustard

Sea salt and ground black pepper, to taste

1 teaspoon olive oil

Directions

Toss the lobster tails with the other Ingredients until they are well coated on all sides.

Cook the lobster tails at 370 degrees F for 3 minutes. Then, turn them and cook on the other side for 3 to 4 minutes more until they are opaque.

Serve warm and enjoy!

Famous Tuna Niçoise Salad

(Ready in about 15 minutes | Servings 3)

Per serving:

315 Calories; 13g Fat; 11.5g Carbs; 37.3g Protein; 3.9g Sugars

Ingredients

1 pound tuna steak

Sea salt and ground black pepper, to taste 1/2 teaspoon red pepper flakes, crushed 1/4 teaspoon dried dill weed

1/2 teaspoon garlic paste

1 pound green beans, trimmed 2 handfuls baby spinach

2 handfuls iceberg lettuce, torn into pieces 1/2 red onion, sliced

1 cucumber, sliced

2 tablespoons lemon juice 1 tablespoon olive oil

1 teaspoon Dijon mustard

1 tablespoon balsamic vinegar

1 tablespoon roasted almonds, coarsely chopped 1 tablespoon fresh parsley, coarsely chopped

Directions

Pat the tuna steak dry; toss your tuna with salt, black pepper, red pepper, dill and garlic paste. Spritz your tuna with a nonstick cooking spray.

Cook the tuna steak at 400 degrees F for 5 minutes; turn your tuna steak over and continue to cook for 4 to 5 minutes more.

Then, add the green beans to the cooking basket. Spritz green beans with a nonstick cooking spray. Cook at 400 degrees F for 5 minutes, shaking the basket once or twice.

Cut your tuna into thin strips and transfer to a salad bowl; add in the green beans.

Then, add in the baby spinach, iceberg lettuce, onion and cucumber and toss to combine. In a mixing bowl, whisk the lemon juice, olive oil, mustard and vinegar.

Dress the salad and garnish with roasted almonds and fresh parsley. Bon appétit!

Fish Cakes with Bell Pepper

(Ready in about 15 minutes | Servings 3)

Per serving:

226 Calories; 6.5g Fat; 10.9g Carbs; 31.4g Protein; 2.6g Sugars

Ingredients

1 pound haddock

1 egg

2 tablespoons milk

1 bell pepper, deveined and finely chopped 2 stalks fresh scallions, minced

1/2 teaspoon fresh garlic, minced

Sea salt and ground black pepper, to taste 1/2 teaspoon cumin seeds

1/4 teaspoon celery seeds

1/2 cup breadcrumbs 1 teaspoon olive oil

Directions

Thoroughly combine all Ingredients, except for the breadcrumbs and olive oil, until everything is blended well.

Then, roll the mixture into 3 patties and coat them with breadcrumbs, pressing to adhere. Drizzle olive oil over the patties and transfer them to the Air Fryer cooking basket.

Cook the fish cakes at 400 degrees F for 5 minutes; turn them over and continue to cook an additional 5 minutes until cooked through.

Bon appétit!

Fish Sticks with Vidalia Onions

(Ready in about 12 minutes | Servings 2)

Per serving:

571 Calories; 41.7g Fat; 36.2g Carbs; 14.2g Protein; 9.2g Sugars

Ingredients

1/2 pound fish sticks, frozen

1/2 pound Vidalia onions, halved 1 teaspoon sesame oil

Sea salt and ground black pepper, to taste 1/2 teaspoon red pepper flakes

4 tablespoons mayonnaise

4 tablespoons Greek-style yogurt 1/4 teaspoon mustard seeds

1 teaspoon chipotle chili in adobo, minced

Directions

Drizzle the fish sticks and Vidalia onions with sesame oil. Toss them with salt, black pepper and red pepper flakes.

Transfer them to the Air Fryer cooking basket.

Cook the fish sticks and onions at 400 degreed F for 5 minutes. Shake the basket and cook an additional 5 minutes or until cooked through.

Meanwhile, mix the mayonnaise, Greek-style yogurt, mustard seeds and chipotle chili.

Serve the warm fish sticks garnished with Vidalia onions and the sauce on the side. Bon appétit!

Fried Oysters with Kaffir Lime Sauce

(Ready in about 10 minutes | Servings 2)

Per serving:

295 Calories; 8.7g Fat; 23.4g Carbs; 30g Protein; 3.3g Sugars

Ingredients

8 fresh oysters, shucked 1/3 cup plain flour

1 egg

3/4 cup breadcrumbs

1/2 teaspoon Italian seasoning mix 1 lime, freshly squeezed

1 teaspoon coconut sugar 1 kaffir lime leaf, shredded 1 habanero pepper, minced 1 teaspoon olive oil

Directions

Clean the oysters and set them aside.

Add the flour to a rimmed plate. Whisk the egg in another rimmed plate. Mix the breadcrumbs and Italian seasoning mix in a third plate.

Dip your oysters in the flour, shaking off the excess. Then, dip them in the egg mixture and finally, coat your oysters with the breadcrumb mixture.

Spritz the breaded oysters with a nonstick cooking spray.

Cook your oysters in the preheated Air Fryer at 400 degrees F for 2 to 3 minutes, shaking the basket halfway through the cooking time.

Meanwhile, blend the remaining Ingredients to make the sauce. Serve the warm oysters with the kaffir lime sauce on the side. Bon appétit!

Garlic Butter Scallops

(Ready in about 10 minutes | Servings 2)

Per serving:

199 Calories; 12.1g Fat; 6.5g Carbs; 14.4g Protein; 1.2g Sugars

Ingredients

1/2 pound scallops

Coarse sea salt and ground black pepper, to taste 1/4 teaspoon cayenne pepper

1/4 teaspoon dried oregano 1/4 teaspoon dried basil

2 tablespoons butter pieces, cold

1 teaspoon garlic, minced 1 teaspoon lemon zest

Directions

Sprinkle the scallops with salt, black pepper, cayenne pepper, oregano and basil. Spritz your scallops with a nonstick cooking oil and transfer them to the Air Fryer cooking basket.

Cook the scallops at 400 degrees F for 6 to 7 minutes, shaking the basket halfway through the cooking time.

In the meantime, melt the butter in a small saucepan over medium-high heat. Once hot, add in the garlic and continue to sauté until fragrant, about 1 minute. Add in lemon zest, taste and adjust the seasonings.

Spoon the garlic butter over the warm scallops and serve.

300. Baked Sardines with Tangy Dipping Sauce

(Ready in about 45 minutes | Servings 3)

Per serving:

413 Calories; 29.1g Fat; 4g Carbs; 32g Protein; 1.7g Sugars

Ingredients

1 pound fresh sardines

Sea salt and ground black pepper, to taste 1 teaspoon Italian seasoning mix

2 cloves garlic, minced 3 tablespoons olive oil

1/2 lemon, freshly squeezed

Directions

Toss your sardines with salt, black pepper and Italian seasoning mix. Cook in your Air Fryer at 325 degrees F for 35 to 40 minutes until skin is crispy.

Meanwhile, make the sauce by whisking the remaining Ingredients Serve warm sardines with the sauce on the side. Bon appétit!

Ginger-Garlic Swordfish with Mushrooms

(Ready in about 15 minutes | Servings 3)

Per serving:

242 Calories; 10.3g Fat; 4.1g Carbs; 32.4g Protein; 2.2g Sugars

Ingredients

1 pound swordfish steak

1 teaspoon ginger-garlic paste

Sea salt and ground black pepper, to taste 1/4 teaspoon cayenne pepper

1/4 teaspoon dried dill weed 1/2 pound mushrooms

Directions

Rub the swordfish steak with ginger-garlic paste; season with salt, black pepper, cayenne pepper and dried dill.

Spritz the fish with a nonstick cooking spray and transfer to the Air Fryer cooking basket. Cook at 400 degrees F for 5 minutes.

Now, add the mushrooms to the cooking basket and continue to cook for 5 minutes longer until tender and fragrant. Eat warm.

Greek Sardeles Psites

(Ready in about 40 minutes | Servings 2)

Per serving:

349 Calories; 17.5g Fat; 19g Carbs; 26.3g Protein; 4.3g Sugars

Ingredients

4 sardines, cleaned

1/4 cup all-purpose flour

Sea salt and ground black pepper, to taste 4 tablespoons extra-virgin olive oil

1/2 red onion, chopped

1/2 teaspoon fresh garlic, minced 1/4 cup sweet white wine

1 tablespoon fresh coriander, minced 1/4 cup baby capers, drained

1 tomato, crushed

1/4 teaspoon chili paper flakes

Directions

Coat your sardines with all-purpose flour until well coated on all sides.

Season your sardines with salt and black pepper and arrange them in the cooking basket. Cook in your Air Fryer at 325 degrees F for 35 to 40 minutes until the skin is crispy.

Meanwhile, heat olive oil in a frying pan over a moderate flame. Now, sauté the onion and garlic for 4 to 5 minutes or until tender and aromatic.

Stir in the remaining Ingredients, cover and let it simmer, for about 15 minutes or until the sauce has thickened and reduced. Spoon the sauce over the warm sardines and serve immediately. Enjoy!

Greek-Style Sea Bass

(Ready in about 15 minutes | Servings 2)

Per serving:

174 Calories; 4.8g Fat; 5g Carbs; 25.8g Protein; 2.6g Sugars

Ingredients

1/2 pound sea bass

1 garlic clove, halved

Sea salt and ground black pepper, to taste 1/2 teaspoon rigani (Greek oregano)

1/2 teaspoon dried dill weed 1/4 teaspoon ground bay leaf 1/4 teaspoon ground cumin 1/2 teaspoon shallot powder Greek sauce:

1/2 Greek yogurt

1 teaspoon olive oil

1/2 teaspoon Tzatziki spice mix 1 teaspoon lime juice

Directions

Pat dry the sea bass with paper towels. Rub the fish with garlic halves.

Toss the fish with salt, black pepper, rigani, dill, ground bay leaf, ground cumin and shallot powder.

Cook the sea bass in your Air Fryer at 400 degrees F for 5 minutes; turn the filets over and cook on the other side for 5 to 6 minutes.

In the meantime, make the sauce by simply blending the remaining Ingredients. Serve the warm fish dolloped with Greek-style sauce. Enjoy!

Grouper with Miso-Honey Sauce

(Ready in about 15 minutes | Servings 2)

Per serving:

331 Calories; 10.7g Fat; 20.7g Carbs; 37.5g Protein; 12.7g Sugars

Ingredients

3/4 pound grouper fillets

Salt and white pepper, to taste 1 tablespoon sesame oil

1 teaspoon water

1 teaspoon deli mustard or Dijon mustard 1/4 cup white miso

1 tablespoon mirin

1 tablespoon honey

1 tablespoon Shoyu sauce

Directions

Sprinkle the grouper fillets with salt and white pepper; drizzle them with a nonstick cooking oil.

Cook the fish at 400 degrees F for 5 minutes; turn the fish fillets over and cook an additional 5 minutes.

Meanwhile, make the sauce by whisking the remaining Ingredients. Serve the warm fish with the miso-honey sauce on the side. Bon appétit!

Haddock Steaks with Decadent Mango Salsa

(Ready in about 15 minutes | Servings 2)

Per serving:

411 Calories; 25.5g Fat; 18.4g Carbs; 26.3g Protein; 14g Sugars

Ingredients

2 haddock steaks

1 teaspoon butter, melted 1 tablespoon white wine

Sea salt and ground black pepper, to taste Mango salsa:

1/2 mango, diced

1/4 cup red onion, chopped

1 chili pepper, deveined and minced 1 teaspoon cilantro, chopped

2 tablespoons fresh lemon juice

Directions

Toss the haddock with butter, wine, salt and black pepper.

Cook the haddock in your Air Fryer at 400 degrees F for 5 minutes. Flip the haddock and cook on the other side for 5 minutes more.

Meanwhile, make the mango salsa by mixing all Ingredients. Serve the warm haddock with the chilled mango salsa and enjoy!

Halibut Steak with Cremini Mushrooms

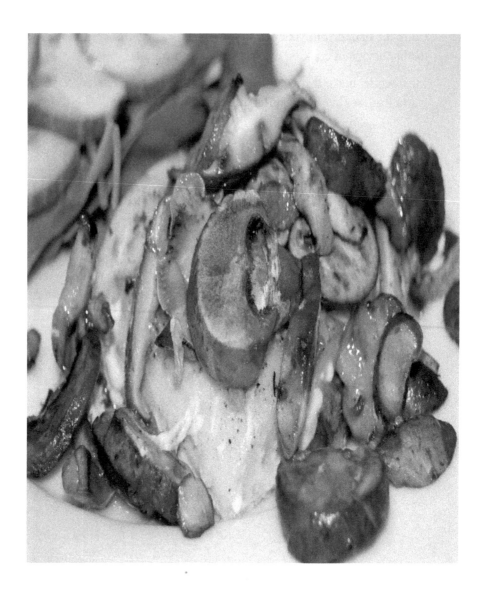

(Ready in about 15 minutes | Servings 3)

Per serving:

326 Calories; 23.7g Fat; 4.2g Carbs; 23.1g Protein; 1.9g Sugars

Ingredients

1 pound halibut steak 1 teaspoon olive oil

Sea salt and ground black pepper, to taste

7 ounces Cremini mushrooms 1 teaspoon butter, melted

1/4 teaspoon onion powder

1/4 teaspoon garlic powder 1/2 teaspoon rosemary

1/2 teaspoon basil

1/2 teaspoon oregano

Directions

Toss the halibut steak with olive oil, salt and black pepper and transfer to the Air Fryer cooking basket.

Toss the Cremini mushrooms with the other Ingredients until well coated on all sides.

Cook the halibut steak at 400 degrees F for 5 minutes. Turn the halibut steak

over and top with mushrooms.

Continue to cook an additional 5 minutes or until the mushrooms are fragrant. Serve warm and enjoy!

Halibut Steak with Zoodles and Lemon

(Ready in about 15 minutes | Servings 3)

Per serving:

341 Calories; 23.1g Fat; 8.2g Carbs; 26.3g Protein; 1.2g Sugars

Ingredients

1 pound halibut steak, cut into 3 pieces 1 garlic clove, halved

1 teaspoon avocado oil

Sea salt and black pepper, to taste 1 pound zucchini, julienned

1/2 teaspoon onion powder

1/2 teaspoon granulated garlic

1 tablespoon fresh parsley, minced 1 teaspoon sage, minced

1 lemon, sliced

Directions

Rub the halibut steaks with garlic and toss with avocado oil, salt and black pepper; then, transfer the halibut steaks to the Air Fryer cooking basket.

Cook the halibut steak at 400 degrees F for 5 minutes. Turn the halibut steak over and continue to cook an additional 5 minutes or until it flakes easily when tested with a fork.

Meanwhile, spritz a wok with a nonstick spray; heat the wok over medium-high heat.

Once hot, stir fry the zucchini noodles along with the onion powder and granulated garlic; cook for 2 to 3 minutes or until just tender.

Top your zoodles with the parsley and sage and stir to combine. Serve the hot zoodles with the halibut steaks and lemon slices. Bon appétit!

Herb and Garlic Grouper Filets

(Ready in about 15 minutes | Servings 3)

Per serving:

184 Calories; 5.4g Fat; 2.5g Carbs; 29.8g Protein; 0.9g Sugars

Ingredients

1 pound grouper filets

1/4 teaspoon shallot powder 1/4 teaspoon porcini powder

1 teaspoon fresh garlic, minced 1/2 teaspoon cayenne pepper 1/2 teaspoon hot paprika

1/4 teaspoon oregano 1/2 teaspoon marjoram 1/2 teaspoon sage

1 tablespoon butter, melted

Sea salt and black pepper, to taste

Directions

Pat dry the grouper filets using kitchen towels.

In a small dish, make the rub by mixing the remaining Ingredients until everything is well incorporated.

Rub the fish with the mixture, coating well on all sides.

Cook the grouper filets in the preheated Air Fryer at 400 degrees F for minutes; turn the filets over and cook on the other side for 5 minutes more. Serve over hot rice if desired. Bon appétit!

Homemade Fish Fingers

(Ready in about 15 minutes | Servings 2)

Per serving:

332 Calories; 10.5g Fat; 12.2g Carbs; 46.3g Protein; 2.8g Sugars

Ingredients

3/4 pound tilapia 1 egg

2 tablespoons milk

4 tablespoons chickpea flour 1/4 cup pork rinds

1/2 cup breadcrumbs

1/2 teaspoon red chili flakes

Coarse sea salt and black pepper, to season

Directions

Rinse the tilapia and pat it dry using kitchen towels. Then, cut the tilapia into strips.

Then, whisk the egg, milk and chickpea flour in a rimmed plate.

Add the pork rinds and breadcrumbs to another plate; stir in red chili flakes, salt and black pepper and stir to combine well.

Dip the fish strips in the egg mixture, then, roll them over the breadcrumb mixture. Transfer the fish fingers to the Air Fryer cooking basket and spritz them with a nonstick cooking spray.

Cook in the preheated Air Fryer at 400 degrees F for 10 minutes, shaking the basket halfway through to ensure even browning. Serve warm and enjoy!

Keto Cod Fillets

(Ready in about 15 minutes | Servings 2)

Per serving:

218 Calories; 12.5g Fat; 3.5g Carbs; 22g Protein; 1.9g Sugars

Ingredients

2 cod fish fillets

1 teaspoon butter, melted

1 teaspoon Old Bay seasoning 1 egg, beaten

2 tablespoons coconut milk, unsweetened 1/3 cup coconut flour, unsweetened

Directions

Place the cod fish fillets, butter and Old Bay seasoning in a Ziplock bag; shake until the fish is well coated on all sides.

In a shallow bowl, whisk the egg and coconut milk until frothy.

In another bowl, place the coconut flour. Dip the fish fillets in the egg mixture, then, coat them with coconut flour, pressing to adhere.

Cook the fish at 390 degrees F for 6 minutes; flip them over and cook an additional 6 minutes until your fish flakes easily when tested with a fork. Bon appétit!

Marinated Flounder Filets

(Ready in about 15 minutes + marinating time | Servings 3)

Per serving:

376 Calories; 14g Fat; 24.5g Carbs; 34.1g Protein; 4.8g Sugars

Ingredients

1 pound flounder filets

1 teaspoon garlic, minced 2 tablespoons soy sauce 1 teaspoon Dijon mustard 1/4 cup malt vinegar

1 teaspoon granulated sugar Salt and black pepper, to taste 1/2 cup plain flour

1 egg

2 tablespoons milk

1/2 cup parmesan cheese, grated

Directions

Place the flounder filets, garlic, soy sauce, mustard, vinegar and sugar in a glass bowl; cover and let it marinate in your refrigerator for at least 1 hour.

Transfer the fish to a plate, discarding the marinade. Salt and pepper to taste.

Place the plain flour in a shallow bowl; in another bowl, beat the egg and milk until pale and well combined; add parmesan cheese to the third bowl.

Dip the flounder filets in the flour, then in the egg mixture; repeat the process and coat them with the parmesan cheese, pressing to adhere.

Cook the flounder filets in the preheated Air Fryer at 400 degrees F for 5 minutes; turn the flounder filets over and cook on the other side for 5 minutes more. Enjoy!

Melt-in-Your Mouth Salmon with Cilantro Sauce

(Ready in about 15 minutes | Servings 2)

Per serving:

419 Calories; 20.2g Fat; 3.2g Carbs; 53.3g Protein; 1.6g Sugars

Ingredients

1 pound salmon fillets 1 teaspoon coconut oil

Sea salt and ground black pepper, to season

2 heaping tablespoons cilantro 1/2 cup Mexican crema

1 tablespoon fresh lime juice

Directions

Rinse and pat your salmon dry using paper towels. Toss the salmon with coconut oil, salt and black pepper.

Cook the salmon filets in your Air Fryer at 380 degrees F for 6 minutes; turn the salmon filets over and cook on the other side for 6 to 7 minutes.

Meanwhile, mix the remaining Ingredients in your blender or food processor. Spoon the cilantro sauce over the salmon filets and serve immediately.

Mom's Lobster Tails

(Ready in about 10 minutes | Servings 2)

Per serving:

256 Calories; 13.7g Fat; 12.7g Carbs; 21.5g Protein; 6.3g Sugars

Ingredients

1/2 pound lobster tails 1 teaspoon olive oil

1 teaspoon fresh lime juice

1 bell pepper, sliced

1 jalapeno pepper, sliced 1 carrot, julienned

1 cup green cabbage, shredded 2 tablespoons mayonnaise

2 tablespoons Greek-style yogurt

Sea salt and ground black pepper, to taste 1 teaspoon baby capers, drained

4 leaves butterhead lettuce, for serving

Directions

Drizzle olive oil over the lobster tails and transfer them to the Air Fryer cooking basket.

Cook the lobster tails at 370 degrees F for 3 minutes. Then, turn them over and cook on the other side for 3 to 4 minutes more until they are opaque.

Toss the lobster tails with the other Ingredients, except for the lettuce leaves; gently stir until well combined.

Lay the lettuce leaves on a serving platter and top with the lobster salad. Bon appétit!

Mom's Toad in the Hole

(Ready in about 45 minutes | Servings 4)

Per serving:

584 Calories; 40.2g Fat; 29.5g Carbs; 23.4g Protein; 3.4g Sugars

Ingredients

6 beef sausages

1 tablespoon butter, melted 1 cup plain flour

A pinch of salt 2 eggs

1 cup semi-skimmed milk

Directions

Cook the sausages in the preheated Air Fryer at 380 degrees F for 15 minutes, shaking halfway through the cooking time.

Meanwhile, make up the batter mix.

Tip the flour into a bowl with salt; make a well in the middle and crack the eggs into it. Mix with an electric whisk; now, slowly and gradually pour in the milk, whisking all the time.

Place the sausages in a lightly greased baking pan. Pour the prepared batter over the sausages.

Cook in the preheated Air Fryer at 370 degrees F approximately 25 minutes, until golden and risen. Serve with gravy if desired. Bon appétit!

Moroccan Harissa Shrimp

(Ready in about 10 minutes | Servings 3)

Per serving:

240 Calories; 5.1g Fat; 20.2g Carbs; 25.2g Protein; 2.3g Sugars

Ingredients

1 pound breaded shrimp, frozen 1 teaspoon extra-virgin olive oil

Sea salt and ground black pepper, to taste

1 teaspoon coriander seeds 1 teaspoon caraway seeds

1 teaspoon crushed red pepper

1 teaspoon fresh garlic, minced

Directions

Toss the breaded shrimp with olive oil and transfer to the Air Fryer cooking basket.

Cook in the preheated Air Fryer at 400 degrees F for 5 minutes; shake the basket and cook an additional 4 minutes.

Meanwhile, mix the remaining Ingredients until well combined. Taste and adjust seasonings. Toss the warm shrimp with the harissa sauce and serve immediately. Enjoy!

Parmesan Chip-Crusted Tilapia

(Ready in about 15 minutes | Servings 3)

Per serving:

356 Calories; 10.5g Fat; 11.9g Carbs; 52g Protein; 2.1g Sugars

Ingredients

1 ½ pounds tilapia, slice into 4 portions Sea salt and ground black pepper, to taste 1/2 teaspoon cayenne pepper

1 teaspoon granulated garlic 1/4 cup almond flour

1/4 cup parmesan cheese, preferably freshly grated

1 egg, beaten

2 tablespoons buttermilk

1 cup tortilla chips, crushed

Directions

Generously season your tilapia with salt, black pepper and cayenne pepper.

Prepare a bread station. Add the granulated garlic, almond flour and parmesan cheese to a rimmed plate.

Whisk the egg and buttermilk in another bowl and place crushed tortilla chips in the third bowl.

Dip the tilapia pieces in the flour mixture, then in the egg/buttermilk mixture and finally roll them in the crushed chips, pressing to adhere well.

Cook in your Air Fryer at 400 degrees F for 10 minutes, flipping halfway through the cooking time. Serve with chips if desired. Bon appétit!

Salmon Bowl with Lime Drizzle

(Ready in about 15 minutes | Servings 3)

Per serving:

307 Calories; 15g Fat; 4.5g Carbs; 32.3g Protein; 5g Sugars

Ingredients

1 pound salmon steak 2 teaspoons sesame oil

Sea salt and Sichuan pepper, to taste

1/2 teaspoon coriander seeds 1 lime, juiced

2 tablespoons reduced-sodium soy sauce

1 teaspoon honey

Directions

Pat the salmon dry and drizzle it with 1 teaspoon of sesame oil.

Season the salmon with salt, pepper and coriander seeds. Transfer the salmon to the Air Fryer cooking basket.

Cook the salmon at 400 degrees F for 5 minutes; turn the salmon over and continue to cook for 5 minutes more or until opaque.

Meanwhile, warm the remaining Ingredients in a small saucepan to make the lime drizzle.

Slice the fish into bite-sized strips, drizzle with the sauce and serve immediately. Enjoy!

Salmon Fillets with Herbs and Garlic

(Ready in about 15 minutes | Servings 3)

Per serving:

248 Calories; 11.2g Fat; 3.1g Carbs; 31.4g Protein; 1.2g Sugars

Ingredients

1 pound salmon fillets

Sea salt and ground black pepper, to taste 1 tablespoon olive oil

1 sprig thyme

2 sprigs rosemary

2 cloves garlic, minced 1 lemon, sliced

Directions

Pat the salmon fillets dry and season them with salt and pepper; drizzle salmon fillets with olive oil and place in the Air Fryer cooking basket.

Cook the salmon fillets at 380 degrees F for 7 minutes; turn them over, top with thyme, rosemary and garlic and continue to cook for 5 minutes more.

Serve topped with lemon slices and enjoy!

Southwestern Prawns with Asparagus

(Ready in about 10 minutes | Servings 3)

Per serving:

280 Calories; 12.1g Fat; 12.8g Carbs; 34.1g Protein; 4g Sugars

Ingredients

1 pound prawns, deveined

1/2 pound asparagus spears, cut into1-inch chinks 1 teaspoon butter, melted

1/4 teaspoon oregano

1/2 teaspoon mixed peppercorns, crushed Salt, to taste

1 ripe avocado

1 lemon, sliced

1/2 cup chunky-style salsa

Directions

Toss your prawns and asparagus with melted butter, oregano, salt and mixed peppercorns.

Cook the prawns and asparagus at 400 degrees F for 5 minutes, shaking the basket halfway through the cooking time.

Divide the prawns and asparagus between serving plates and garnish with avocado and lemon slices. Serve with the salsa on the side. Bon appétit!

Thai-Style Jumbo Scallops

(Ready in about 40 minutes | Servings 2)

Per serving:

200 Calories; 10.5g Fat; 10.2g Carbs; 16.3g Protein; 3.4g Sugars

Ingredients

8 jumbo scallops

1 teaspoon sesame oil

Sea salt and red pepper flakes, to season 1 tablespoon coconut oil

1 Thai chili, deveined and minced 1 teaspoon garlic, minced

1 tablespoon oyster sauce 1 tablespoon soy sauce 1/4 cup coconut milk

2 tablespoons fresh lime juice

Directions

Pat the jumbo scallops dry and toss them with 1 teaspoon of sesame oil, salt and red pepper.

Cook the jumbo scallops in your Air Fryer at 400 degrees F for 4 minutes; turn them over and cook an additional 3 minutes.

While your scallops are cooking, make the sauce in a frying pan. Heat the coconut oil in a pan over medium-high heat.

Once hot, cook the Thai chili and garlic for 1 minute or so until just tender and fragrant. Add in the oyster sauce, soy sauce and coconut milk and continue to simmer, partially covered, for 5 minutes longer.

Lastly, stir in fresh lime juice and stir to combine well. Add the warm scallops to the sauce and serve immediately.

Alphabetical index

CPSIA information can be obtained
at www.ICGtesting.com
Printed in the USA
BVHW041401040521
606417BV00001B/139

9 781802 834314